Pebble® Plus

Sharks

Whale Shark

by Deborah Nuzzolo

Consulting Editor: Gail Saunders-Smith, PhD

Consultant: Jody Rake, member
Southwest Marine/Aquatic Educators' Association

Capstone press®

Mankato, Minnesota

Pebble Plus is published by Capstone Press,
151 Good Counsel Drive, P.O. Box 669, Mankato, Minnesota 56002.
www.capstonepress.com

1 2 3 4 5 6 13 12 11 10 09 08

Library of Congress Cataloging-in-Publication Data
Nuzzolo, Deborah.
    Whale shark / by Deborah Nuzzolo.
    p. cm. — (Pebble plus. Sharks)
    Includes bibliographical references and index.
    Summary: "Simple text and photographs present whale sharks, their body parts,
and their behavior" — Provided by publisher.
    ISBN-13: 978-1-4296-1731-4 (hardcover)
    ISBN-10: 1-4296-1731-4 (hardcover)
    1. Whale shark — Juvenile literature. I. Title.
QL638.95.R4N89 2009
597.3 — dc22   2007051314

Editorial Credits
Megan Peterson, editor; Ted Williams, set designer; Kyle Grenz, book designer; Jo Miller, photo researcher

Photo Credits
Dreamstime/Harald Bolten, 1
Getty Images Inc./Minden Pictures/D. P. Wilson/FLPA, 17; National Geographic/Brian Skerry, 4–5; Taxi/Gary
    Bell, 19
iStockphoto   ngbeek-van Kranen, 7
Nature P   rary/Jurgen Freund, 9
Peter A   reund, 14–15, 20–21; Kelvin Aitken, 10–11, 13
Shutt   one Conti, backgrounds
                /Pacific Stock, cover

Note to Parents and Teachers

rks set supports national science standards related to the characteristics and
or of animals. This book describes and illustrates whale sharks. The images
early readers in understanding the text. The repetition of words and phrases
early readers learn new words. This book also introduces early readers to
specific vocabulary words, which are defined in the Glossary section. Early
rs may need assistance to read some words and to use the Table of Contents,
sary, Read More, Internet Sites, and Index sections of the book.

Table of Contents

Not a Whale

Whale sharks are big,
but they aren't whales.
They are the largest fish
in the world.

Whale sharks swim

in warm, shallow seas.

They travel alone

or in groups called schools.

Whale Shark Pups

Whale shark pups hatch

from eggs inside the mother.

They live and grow

on their own.

What They Look Like

Whale sharks have light spots and dark lines on their backs.

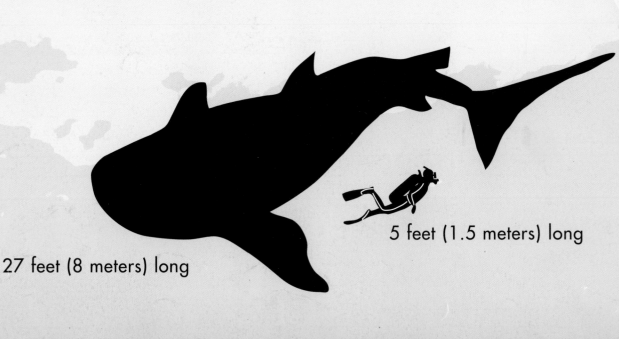

27 feet (8 meters) long

5 feet (1.5 meters) long

11

A whale shark's large mouth
is full of tiny teeth.
The shark has 300 rows
of teeth.

teeth

A whale shark's skeleton

bends easily.

It's made of cartilage.

Cartilage is softer than bone.

Eating

Whale sharks eat small fish,
squid, and plankton.
Plankton are tiny sea plants
and animals.

plankton

17

Whale sharks pull water
into their mouths.
They squeeze the water out
through gills that trap food.

19

Divers can swim
with whale sharks.
These gentle giants
are not dangerous to people.

Glossary

cartilage — the strong, rubbery body tissue that makes up most of a shark's skeleton; a person's nose and ears are also made of cartilage.

dangerous — not safe

gentle — not harmful

giant — a very large creature

gill — a body part that a fish uses to breathe; whale sharks also use their gills to trap food.

hatch — to break out of an egg

plankton — tiny plants and animals that drift or float in oceans and lakes

pup — a young shark

school — a group of fish; as many as 100 whale sharks might gather in a school.

Read More

Crossingham, John, and Bobbie Kalman. *The Life Cycle of a Shark.* The Life Cycle Series. New York: Crabtree, 2006.

Lindeen, Carol K. *Sharks.* Under the Sea. Mankato, Minn.: Capstone Press, 2005.

Thomson, Sarah L. *Amazing Sharks!* An I Can Read Book. New York: HarperCollins, 2005.

Internet Sites

FactHound offers a safe, fun way to find Internet sites related to this book. All of the sites on FactHound have been researched by our staff.

Here's how:

1. Visit *www.facthound.com*

2. Choose your grade level.

3. Type in this book ID **1429617314** for age-appropriate sites. You may also browse subjects by clicking on letters, or by clicking on pictures and words.

4. Click on the **Fetch It** button.

FactHound will fetch the best sites for you!

Index

Word Count: 136

Grade: 1

Early-Intervention Level: 20